FATHERS
A Loving Tribute

FATHERS
A Loving Tribute

Edited by Elizabeth Robbins
Designed by Liz Trovato

GLORYA HALE BOOKS
NEW YORK · AVENEL

For Arthur

The following illustrations were used with
permission from The Bettmann Archive:
Marriage of Princess Elizabeth; Portrait of Aaron Burr;
Queen Victoria and Family; Portrait of Mark Twain;
Mark Twain with Daughters; Theodore Roosevelt with His Sons

This 1996 edition is published by Glorya Hale Books,
an imprint of Random House Value Publishing, Inc.,
40 Engelhard Avenue, Avenel, New Jersey 07001.

Editorial supervision: Carol Kelly Gangi
Production supervision: Ellen Reed

Random House
New York • Toronto • London • Sydney • Auckland

Printed and bound in Singapore

Library of Congress Cataloging-in-Publication Data
Fathers: a loving tribute /
edited by Elizabeth Robbins.
p. cm.
ISBN 0-517-15007-7
1. Fathers and sons—Literary collections.
2. Fathers and daughters—Literary collections.
3. Family—Literary collections.
I. Robbins, Elizabeth.
PN6071.F3F37 1996
808.8'0353—dc20   95-45460
CIP

8 7 6 5 4 3 2 1

INTRODUCTION

Fathers have always been awe-inspiring figures; that is, perhaps, because until fairly recently they have neither consented, nor been forced, to become actively involved in the day-to-day upbringing of their children. Nevertheless, their influence on their sons and daughters has always been strong and novelists and dramatists, as well as poets, have long been inspired to explore these relationships. Many of the world's outstanding leaders in every field of endeavor have heaped praise on their own fathers and many famous men have written of their admiration for their children and of the joys of being fathers. In memorable words, by such distinguished men and women as Mark Twain, Aldous Huxley, Harry Golden, Lafcadio Hearn, Adrienne Rich, Ann Sexton, Henry James, Sr., Louisa May Alcott, and Abraham Lincoln, and with evocative paintings and photographs, *Fathers* pays loving tribute to fathers and to fatherhood.

Included are men's descriptions of their own experiences of being fathers. Christopher Morley, for example, tells of his emotions as he stood next to the crib of his new baby. Henry Wadsworth Longfellow extols his young daughters in his classic poem "The Children's Hour." King George VI of England writes to his daughter, the then Princess Elizabeth, of his feelings on her wedding day. And President Theodore Roosevelt, who wrote many wonderful letters to each of his six children, describes in a note to his third child, Kermit, his activities as "vice-mother" while his wife is away.

Men and women talk about their fathers and the influence they had on their own lives. Cicero, Roman consul, orator, and writer, proclaims, "I am pleased to be praised by a man so praised as you, Father." Margaret Bourke White remembers the nature walks she took with her father, an unusually silent man who became suddenly communicative in the world of out-of-doors. Benjamin Franklin writes about mealtimes at his father's table. And Mario Cuomo and Will Rogers, Jr., explain what they learned from their fathers.

This tribute to fathers was compiled and designed to be a gift of love and will certainly be enjoyed and treasured by every father who receives it.

ELIZABETH ROBBINS
NEW YORK CITY, 1996

I AM PLEASED

TO BE PRAISED BY A MAN SO PRAISED

AS YOU, FATHER.

CICERO, ROMAN CONSUL, ORATOR,
AND WRITER IN THE FIRST CENTURY B.C.

*L*ast night my child *was born*— a very strong boy, with large black eyes. . . . If you ever become a father, I think the strangest and strongest sensation of your life will be hearing for the first time the thin cry of your own child. For a moment you have the strange feeling of being double; but there is something more, quite impossible to analyze—perhaps the echo in a man's heart of all the sensations felt by all the fathers and mothers of his race at a similar instant in the past. It is a very tender, but also a very ghostly feeling.

LAFCADIO HEARN,
NINETEENTH-CENTURY
BRITISH-JAPANESE WRITER

When one becomes a father,

then first one becomes a son. Standing by the crib of one's own baby, with that world-old pang of compassion and protectiveness toward this so little creature that has all its course to run, the heart flies back in yearning and gratitude to those who felt just so toward one's self. Then for the first time one understands the homely succession of sacrifices and pains by which life is transmitted and fostered down the stumbling generations of men.

CHRISTOPHER MORLEY,
TWENTIETH-CENTURY AMERICAN WRITER

*N*o man can possibly know what life means, what the world means, what anything means, until he has a child and loves it. And then the whole universe changes and nothing will ever again seem exactly as it seemed before.

LAFCADIO HEARN

I F THE NEW
AMERICAN FATHER FEELS
BEWILDERED AND EVEN DEFEATED,
LET HIM TAKE COMFORT FROM THE
FACT THAT WHATEVER HE DOES IN
ANY FATHERING SITUATION
HAS A FIFTY PERCENT CHANCE OF
BEING RIGHT.

BILL COSBY,
AMERICAN ACTOR AND WRITER,
IN *FATHERHOOD*

I TURNED THE KNOB AND THE DOOR SWUNG

inward. I raised my eyes, steeled not to anticipate too much, prepared to be initially rejected, ready for disappointment. The room had a green shag carpet and strewn across it were toy trucks and blocks. A small boy, dressed from head to foot in a red zipped-up snowsuit, bent over them. He was not at first aware of my presence and went on with his play, but then he seemed to catch some unexpected echo. He looked up and met my eyes. His face was perfect, deeply etched with dark, narrow eyes, bright beneath thick, straight lashes and brows. Black hair feathered under the ruff of his snowsuit. His mouth was wide, his expression measuring. And then he lit up with recognition. "Hi, Daddy," he said, and, without a beat of strangeness or doubt, went back to his trucks. I stood —stunned, blessed, transported, forever changed—listening with rapt attention to his sounds of screeching brakes and revving engines.

MICHAEL DORRIS,
TWENTIETH-CENTURY AMERICAN WRITER
IN *THE BROKEN CORD*

Be kind to thy father, for when

thou were young,

Who loved thee as fondly as he?

He caught the first accents that

fell from thy tongue,

And joined in thy innocent glee.

MARGARET COURTNEY,
NINETEENTH-CENTURY
AMERICAN POET

My father was an abnormally silent man. He was so absorbed in his own engineering work that he seldom talked to us children at all, but he would become communicative in the world of out-of-doors. . . . I treasured the nature walks Father and I took together. Father could hide in the bushes and whistle bird calls so convincingly that the birds he imitated came to him. He taught me the names of the stars, and how to distinguish the harmless snakes and pick them up without fear.

MARGARET BOURKE WHITE,
TWENTIETH-CENTURY PHOTOGRAPHER
ABOUT HER FATHER, AN INVENTOR

To show a child what has once delighted you, to find the child's delight added to your own, so there is now a double delight seen in the glow of trust and affection, this is happiness.

J. B. PRIESTLEY,
TWENTIETH-CENTURY ENGLISH NOVELIST,
CRITIC, AND PLAYWRIGHT

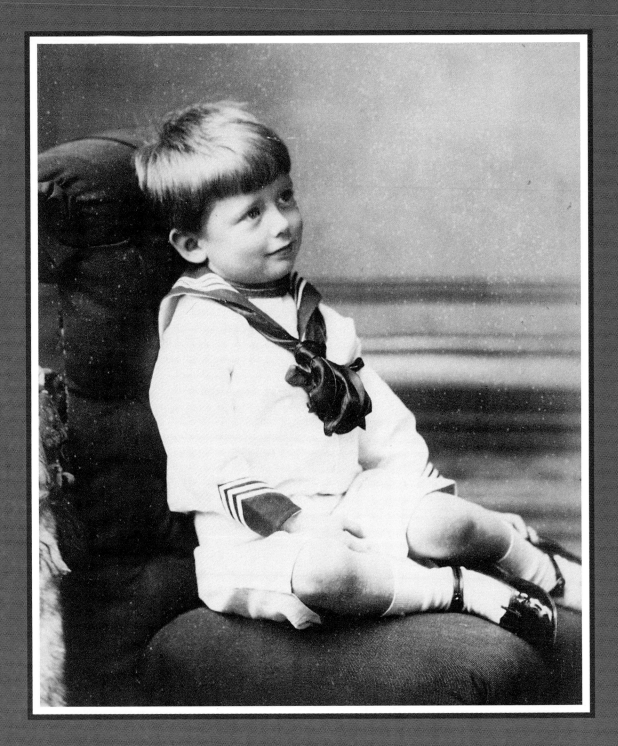

OUR SON

EDGAR A. GUEST,
TWENTIETH-CENTURY AUTHOR OF MANY
VOLUMES OF POPULAR POETRY

He's supposed to be our son, our hope and our pride,

In him all the dreams of our future abide,

But whenever some act to his credit occurs

I never am mentioned, the glory is hers,

And whenever he's bad or has strayed from the line,

Then always she speaks of the rascal as mine.

When trouble has come she will soberly say:

"Do you know what your son has been up to today?

Your son spilled the ink on the living-room floor!

Your son broke the glass in the dining-room door!

I am telling you now something has to be done,

It is high time you started correcting your son!"

But when to the neighbors she boasts of his worth,

It is: "My son's the best little boy on the earth!"

Accuse him of mischief, she'll just floor you flat

With: "My son, I'm certain, would never do that!

Of course there are times when he's willfully bad

But then it's that temper he gets from his dad!"

WHEN MY MOTHER BECAME

pregnant with my brother early in 1951, the year after I was born, Dad was working for a construction company in the Bronx. In early December, on Sunday morning, Mom went into labor. That night Dad called his boss. He was taking paternity leave for two weeks, he said. Dad might as well have told him he was a communist.

STEPHEN BARLAS,
TWENTIETH-CENTURY AMERICAN WRITER,
IN *FROM THE HEARTS OF MEN*

$\mathcal{H}$e is an extraordinarily fine looking man. He is the loveliest man I ever saw or hope to see.

SUSY CLEMENS, MARK TWAIN'S
DAUGHTER, IN HER BIOGRAPHY OF HER
FATHER, WHICH SHE BEGAN WHEN SHE WAS
THIRTEEN YEARS OLD

Mark Twain with his middle daughter and Susy, his eldest

*T*he *impression* the father makes on his son's friends . . . is important enough to leave eradicable scars. Take the time the kid is playing in the street with his friends, and let one of the other kids say, *"Johnny, here comes your father."* Now you have one of the most important moments in a boy's life. Do you have any idea what goes through his mind during that fleeting moment? Your appearance, your dress, your walk, your manner, what you say to your son in greeting, and what you say to the other kids; these are matters of life and death to the son, whose heart thumps wildly throughout the ordeal. Of course, this is something he will never discuss with you. You'll *never* find out from him. You must discover it yourself.

HARRY GOLDEN, TWENTIETH-CENTURY
AMERICAN EDITOR, ESSAYIST, AND BIOGRAPHER,
IN *ONLY IN AMERICA*

IN MY BOYHOOD, I NEVER HAD A DOUBT

that the beliefs they taught me were true. The difficulty was to live up to them and to love God. . . . I believed in the Bible. Creation, to me, meant a Creator. And since there was someone so great and powerful that He has created us all, I felt I had better learn his wishes. . . . I wanted to live in harmony with Him—no small battle of wills. Yet I also wished greatly to get away and live as I liked. . . . I thought of God as a strangely emotional being. He was powerful; He was forgiving yet obdurate, full of wrath and affection. Both his wrath and affection were fitful, they came and they went, and I couldn't count on either to continue; although they both always did. In short God was much such a being as my father himself. What was the relation between them, I wondered—these two puzzling deities?

CLARENCE DAY,
TWENTIETH-CENTURY AMERICAN ESSAYIST
AND ARTIST, IN *GOD AND MY FATHER*

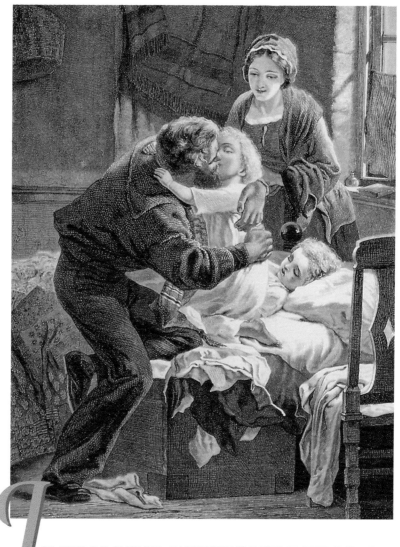

*I*F YOU LIVE WITHOUT BEING A
FATHER YOU WILL DIE WITHOUT
BEING A HUMAN BEING.

RUSSIAN PROVERB

My Enthusiasm for Sports and

Inattention to Books, allarmed my Father, and he frequently entered into conversation with me upon the Subject. I told him [I did not] love Books and wished he would lay aside the thoughts of sending me to Colledge. What would you do Child? Be a Farmer. A Farmer? Well I will shew you what it is to be a Farmer. You shall go with me to Penny ferry tomorrow Morning and help me get Thatch. I shall be very glad to go Sir. —Accordingly next morning he took me with him, and with great good humour kept me all day with him at Work. At night at home he said Well John are you satisfied with being a Farmer. Though the Labour had been very hard and very muddy I answered I like it very well Sir. Ay but I dont like it so well: so you shall go to School to day. I went but was not so happy as at the Creek Thatch.

JOHN ADAMS,
GEORGE WASHINGTON'S VICE-PRESIDENT
AND THE SECOND PRESIDENT OF THE UNITED STATES,
IN HIS AUTOBIOGRAPHY

Alexander Cassatt and His Son Robert by Mary Cassatt

I CANNOT THINK

OF ANY NEED IN CHILDHOOD

AS STRONG AS THE NEED FOR

A FATHER'S PROTECTION.

SIGMUND FREUD (1856-1939)
THE FATHER OF PSYCHOANALYSIS

BLESSED INDEED IS THE MAN WHO
HEARS MANY GENTLE VOICES CALL HIM FATHER!

LYDIA M. CHILD, NINETEENTH-CENTURY AMERICAN
ABOLITIONIST, WRITER, AND EDITOR

WHAT GREATER ORNAMENT TO A SON THAN A FATHER'S GLORY, OR TO A FATHER THAN A SON'S HONORABLE CONDUCT?

SOPHOCLES, GREEK TRAGIC PLAYWRIGHT
IN THE FIRST CENTURY B.C.

A Boy
and His Dad

A boy and his dad on a fishing trip—

There is a glorious fellowship!

Father and son and the open sky

And the white clouds lazily drifting by,

And the laughing stream as it runs along

With the clicking reel like a martial song,

And the father teaching the youngster gay

How to land a fish in the sportsman's way.

Which is happier, man or boy?

The soul of the father is steeped in joy,

For he's finding out, to his heart's delight,

That his son is fit for the future fight.

He is learning the glorious depths of him,

And the thoughts he thinks and his every whim,

And he shall discover, when night comes on,

How close he has grown to his little son.

A boy and his dad on a fishing trip—

Oh, I envy them, as I see them there

Under the sky in the open air,

For out of the old, old long ago

Come the summer days that I used to know,

When I learned life's truths from my father's lips

As I shared the joy of his fishing trips—

Builders of life's companionship!

EDGAR A. GUEST

It gives me the greatest pleasure

to know that you have discovered the charms of my boy. I never boasted his good qualities to you because I thought you would set it down as a father's fondness, but now that you have found them out yourself, I may say that a more intelligent boy, with a sweeter disposition, does not exist in the world. He is besides noble-minded, honest, and true.

LORD WILLIAM RUSSELL,
ENGLISH STATESMAN, TO LADY HOLLAND,
FAMOUS HOSTESS AND GREAT WIT OF
NINETEENTH-CENTURY LONDON

Y

OU ARE TRULY

MY SON, AND NOT ONLY MY SON,

BUT WELL-NIGH THE ONLY HAPPINESS

AND DISTRACTION THAT

I HAVE.

ALEXANDRE DUMAS,
NINTEENTH-CENTURY FRENCH NOVELIST, IN A
LETTER TO HIS NATURAL AND ONLY SON ALEXANDRE

When Theodore Roosevelt became President he moved into the White House with his six children, Alice, Theodore, Kermit, Ethel, Archibald, and Quentin. (The five youngest were fondly called "the White House Gang," and overran the presidential mansion with their playmates. (Kermit, the third oldest was born in 1889.) The letters that follow are only a few of the many he wrote to his children.

Theodore Roosevelt in 1902, during his presidency, with his four sons, Theodore Jr., Kermit, Quentin, and Archibald

Dear Kermit:

Didn't I tell you about Hector, Brier and Sailor Boy (dogs) when I saw them on election day? They were in excellent health, lying around the door of Seaman's house, which they had evidently adopted as their own. Sailor Boy and Brier were exceedingly affectionate; Hector kindly, but uninterested.

Mother has gone off for nine days, and as usual I am acting as vice-mother. Archie and Quentin are really too cunning for anything. Each night I spend about three-quarters of an hour reading to them. I first of all read some book like Algonquin Indian Tales, or the poetry of Scott or Macaulay. Once I read them Jim Bludsoe, which perfectly enthralled them and made Quentin ask me at least a hundred questions. . . . I have also been reading them each evening from the Bible. It has been the story of Saul, David and Jonathan. They have been so interested that several times I have had to read them more than one chapter. Then each says his prayers and repeats the hymn he is learning, Quentin usually jiggling solemnly up and down while he repeats it. Each finally got one hymn perfect, whereupon in accordance with previous instructions from mother I presented each of them with a five-cent piece. Yesterday (Saturday) I took both of them and Ethel, together with the three elder Garfield boys, for a long scramble down Rock Creek. We really had great fun.

White House, April 1, 1906

Darling Quenty-Quee:

Slipper and the kittens are doing finely. I think the kittens will be big enough for you to pet and have some satisfaction out of when you get home, although they will be pretty young still. I miss you all dreadfully, and the house feels big and lonely and full of echoes with nobody but me in it; and I do not hear any small scamps running up and down the hall just as hard as they can; or hear their voices while I am dressing; or suddenly look out through the windows of the office at the tennis ground and see them racing over it or playing in the sand-box. I love you very much.

*W*hen I was a boy of fourteen, my father was so ignorant I could hardly stand to have the old man around. But when I got to be twenty-one, I was astounded at how much he had learned in seven years.

MARK TWAIN
(SAMUEL LANGHORNE CLEMENS)
NINETEENTH-CENTURY AMERICAN
HUMORIST, WRITER, NEWSPAPERMAN,
AND LECTURER

Sons have

Always a rebellious wish

to be disillusioned by that which

charmed their fathers.

Aldous Huxley,
twentieth-century English novelist
and critic

O

NE FATHER

IS MORE THAN

A HUNDRED SCHOOLMASTERS.

ENGLISH PROVERB

Reflected Image by Carl Larsson

October 4, 1738

My Dear Child:

By my writing so often, and by the manner in which I write, you will easily see that I do not treat you as a little child, but as a boy who lives to learn, and is ambitious of receiving instructions. I am even persuaded, that, in reading my letters, you are attentive, not only on the subject of which they treat, but likewise to the orthography and to the style. It is of the greatest importance to write letters well; as this is a talent which unavoidably occurs every day of one's life, as well in business as in pleasure; and inaccuracies in orthography or in style are never pardoned but in ladies. When you are older, you will read the "Epistles" (that is to say Letters) of Cicero; they are the most perfect models of good writing. *A propos* Cicero I must give you some account of him. . . .

In case there should be any words in my letters which you do not perfectly understand, remember always to inquire the explanation from your mamma, or else to seek for them in the dictionary. Adieu.

LORD CHESTERFIELD, EIGHTEENTH-CENTURY ENGLISH STATESMAN AND MAN OF
LETTERS, WROTE ALMOST EVERY DAY TO HIS NATURAL SON PHILIP STANHOPE.
THIS LETTER WAS WRITTEN WHEN PHILIP WAS TEN.

AT MY FATHER'S TABLE HE LIKED TO HAVE,

as often as he could, some sensible friend or neighbor to converse with, and always took care to start some ingenious or useful topic for discourse, which might tend to improve the minds of his children. By this means he turned our attention to what was good, just, and prudent in the conduct of life; and little or no notice was ever taken of what related to the victuals on the table, whether it was well or ill dressed, in or out of season, of good or bad flavor, preferable or inferior to this or that other thing of the kind, so that I was bro't up in such a perfect inattention to these matters as to be quite indifferent to what kind of food was set before me, and so unobservant of it that to this day if I am asked I can scarcely tell a few hours after dinner what I dined upon.

BENJAMIN FRANKLIN,
EIGHTEENTH-CENTURY AMERICAN STATESMAN, SCIENTIST,
AND PHILOSOPHER, IN HIS AUTOBIOGRAPHY

A FATHER IS A BANKER

PROVIDED BY NATURE.

FRENCH PROVERB

Queen Victoria and Albert, in 1848, with five of their children

*N*ONE OF YOU CAN *EVER* BE PROUD

enough of being the *child* of SUCH a Father who has not his *equal* in this world—so great, so good, so faultless. Try, all of you, to follow in his footsteps and don't be discouraged, for to be *really* in everything like him *none* of you, I am sure, will ever be. Try, therefore, to be like him in *some* points, and you will have *acquired a great deal.*

QUEEN VICTORIA
IN A LETTER OF AUGUST 26, 1857, TO THE PRINCE OF WALES,
LATER KING EDWARD VII, THE SECOND OF HER NINE CHILDREN

M Y MOST HUMBLE THANKS FOR THE

many fine things that you have bestowed on me. And though

they be my greatest ornaments . . . they could not give me any

contentment, but as I understand they are expressions of your

Lordship's favor; a blessing that, above all others in this world, I

do with most passion desire.

LADY DOROTHY SIDNEY (1617–1684),
LATER COUNTESS OF SUNDERLAND, TO HER FATHER
THE EARL OF LEICESTER

I

NEVER SAW ONE

SO FITTED BY HER GRACE

AND PLAYFULNESS AND WIT

TO ADORN THIS LIFE.

HENRY JAMES,
NINETEENTH-CENTURY AMERICAN PHILOSOPHER
AND WRITER, ABOUT HIS DAUGHTER ALICE,
THE BRILLIANT YOUNGER SISTER OF
WILLIAM AND HENRY JAMES

HE IS THE HAPPIEST,

BE HE KING OR PEASANT,

WHO FINDS PEACE IN

HIS HOME.

JOHANN WOLFGANG VON GOETHE,
EIGHTEENTH-CENTURY GERMAN POET

THE COMPANION,

the friend, and confidant of her mother,

and the object of a pleasure something like

the love between the angels to her father.

RICHARD STEELE,
EIGHTEENTH-CENTURY ENGLISH WRITER

*Y*ou appear to me so superior, so elevated above other men. I contemplate you with such a strange mixture of humility, admiration, reverence, love, and pride, that very little superstition would be necessary to make me worship you as a superior being. . . . I had rather not live than not be the daughter of such a man.

THEODOSIA BURR,
IN A LETTER TO HER FATHER
AARON BURR, THE AMERICAN
REVOLUTIONARY OFFICER AND POLITICAL
LEADER WHO BECAME THE THIRD VICE
PRESIDENT OF THE UNITED STATES

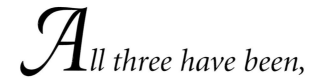

*A*ll three have been,

and continue to be, the joy of my life, and of the many pieces

of good fortune that have been poured out on me

I count this as the greatest.

KENNETH CLARK,
TWENTIETH-CENTURY ENGLISH ART HISTORIAN,
ABOUT HIS CHILDREN

THEY WERE ALL VERY

young and gay and handsome and happy, and they

unknowingly provided one of those rare occasions

when one can see in one glance that all the hideous

sacrifices entailed in their education have not so far

been wasted.

RUPERT HART-DAVIS,
TWENTIETH-CENTURY BRITISH PUBLISHER AND EDITOR,
ABOUT HIS CHILDREN, AFTER A FAMILY REUNION

THE CHILDREN'S HOUR

Between the dark and the daylight,
  When the night is beginning to lower,
Comes a pause in the day's occupations,
  That is known as the children's hour.

I hear in the chamber above me
  The patter of little feet,
The sound of a door that is opened,
  And voices soft and sweet.

From my study I see in the lamplight,
  Descending the broad hall stair,
Grave Alice, and laughing Allegra,
  And Edith with golden hair.

A whisper, and then a silence:
  Yet I know, by their merry eyes
They are plotting and planning together
  To take me by surprise.

A sudden rush from the stairway,
  A sudden raid from the hall!
By three doors left unguarded
  They enter my castle wall!

Longfellow's three daughters

They climb up into my turret
　　O'er the arms and back of my chair;
If I try to escape, they surround me;
　　They seem to be everywhere.

They almost devour me with kisses,
　　Their arms about me entwine,
Till I think of the Bishop of Bingen
　　In his Mouse-Tower on the Rhine!

Do you think, O blue-eyed banditti,
　　Because you have scaled the wall,
Such an old mustache as I am
　　Is not a match for you all!

I have you fast in my fortress,
　　And will not let you depart,
But put you down into the dungeon
　　In the round tower of my heart.

And there will I keep you forever,
　　Yes, forever and a day,
Till the walls shall crumble to ruin,
　　And molder in dust away.

HENRY WADSWORTH LONGFELLOW,
NINETEENTH-CENTURY AMERICAN POET,
WROTE THIS FAMOUS POEM FOR HIS
THREE DAUGHTERS

I WAS SO PROUD OF YOU

and thrilled at having you so close to

me on our long walk in Westminster

Abbey, but when I handed your hand to

the Archbishop I felt I had lost something

very precious.

GEORGE VI OF ENGLAND,
IN A LETTER TO HIS DAUGHTER PRINCESS ELIZABETH
JUST AFTER HER MARRIAGE TO PHILIP MOUNTBATTEN
ON NOVEMBER 20, 1947

AMONGST THE OTHER INNUMERABLE

blessings, I must not forget the bounty of Heaven in granting you a mind

that rejoices in the practice of those eminent virtues which form great and

good characters. . . . The height of glory to which your professional judge-

ment, united with a proper degree of bravery, guarded by Providence, has

raised you, few sons, my dear child, attain to, and few fathers live to see.

EDMOND NELSON,
A PARISH VICAR IN A LETTER TO HIS SON
HORATIO WHO HAD JUST BECOME A
NATIONAL HERO AFTER THE BATTLE OF
ST. VINCENT IN 1797

I do not ask for long letters,

nor care a farthing about choice phrases.

Tell me your domestic news and you will

always do me a great happiness.

SIR WALTER SCOTT (1771-1832),
SCOTTISH ROMANTIC NOVELIST AND POET, TO HIS
MUCH LOVED DAUGHTER-IN-LAW

THIRTY-FOUR YEARS OF UNBROKEN kindness, of cloudless sunshine, of perpetual joy, of constant love. Thirty-four years of happy smiles, of loving looks and gentle words, of generous deeds. Thirty-four years, a flower, a palm, a star, a faultless child, a perfect woman, wife, and mother.

ROBERT G. INGERSOLL,
NINETEENTH-CENTURY AMERICAN LECTURER,
IN A NOTE TO HIS DAUGHTER EVA
ON HER BIRTHDAY

I have infinite faith

in your innate judgement of yourself and your capabilities.

I think you're fortunate in having a sort of in-built gyroscope

which . . . does instinctively give you your bearings

and your balance.

KENNETH ALLSOP,
ENGLISH NATURALIST, FILMMAKER AND WRITER,
TO HIS TWENTY-YEAR-OLD DAUGHTER AMANDA

Abraham Lincoln and his son Tad

Abraham and Mary Lincoln had four sons, of whom two died when they were very young. In 1864, when Robert Lincoln, the eldest, graduated from Harvard Law School, his mother, with two sons already in the grave, was frantic about his determination to enlist. Finally, on January 19, 1865, the President sent this rather apologetic letter to General Ulysses S. Grant:

Lieut. General Grant:

   Please read and answer this letter as though I was not President, but only a friend. My son, now in his twenty-second year, having graduated at Harvard, wishes to see something of the war before it ends. I do not wish to put him in the ranks, nor yet to give him a commission, to which those who have already served long are better entitled, and better qualified to hold. Could he, without embarrassment to you, or detriment to the service, go into your Military family with some nominal rank, I, and not the public, furnishing his necessary means? If no, say so without the least hesitation, because I am as anxious, and as deeply interested, that you shall not be encumbered as you can be yourself. Yours truly,

A. Lincoln

Grant readily consented and, less than a month later, Robert became an assistant adjutant general with the rank of captain. Thomas Lincoln, who was known as Tad, was Lincoln's favorite and survived him. But of the four sons only Robert lived to adulthood.

I

T DOESN'T MATTER WHO MY FATHER WAS; IT MATTERS WHO I REMEMBER HE WAS.

ANNE SEXTON,
TWENTIETH-CENTURY AMERICAN POET

I wanted him to cherish and approve of me, not as he had when I was a child, but as the woman I was, who had her own mind and had made her own choices.

ADRIENNE RICH,
TWENTIETH-CENTURY POET,
IN *BLOOD, BREAD, AND POETRY*

*T*o me,
the saddest sight *I* saw in that sad place, was

the spectacle of a gray-haired father, sitting hour after

hour by his son, dying from the poison of his wound.

The old father, hale and hearty; the young son, past

all help, though one could scarcely believe it; for the

subtle fever, burning his strength away, flushed his

cheeks with color, filled his eyes with luster, and lent

a mournful mockery of health to face and figure,

making the poor lad comelier in death than in life.

His bed was not in my ward; but I was in and out,

and, for a day or two, the pair were much together,

saying little, but looking much. The old man tried to

busy himself with book or pen, that his presence

might not be a burden; and once when he sat writing,

to the anxious mother at home, doubtless, I saw the

son's eyes fixed upon his face, with a look of mingled

resignation and regret, as if trying to teach himself to

say cheerfully the long good-bye. And again, when

the son slept, the father watched him, as he had him-

self been watched; and though no feature of his grave

countenance changed, the rough hand, smoothing

the lock of hair upon the pillow, the bowed attitude

of the gray head, were more pathetic than the loudest

lamentations.

LOUISA MAY ALCOTT,
NINETEENTH-CENTURY AMERICAN WRITER,
IN *HOSPITAL SKETCHES*, BASED UPON HER JOURNAL ENTRIES WHEN
SHE WORKED AS A VOLUNTEER NURSE DURING THE CIVIL WAR

HIS HERITAGE

to his children wasn't words or posses-

sions, but an unspoken treasure, the

treasure of his example as a man and a

father. More than anything I have, I'm

trying to pass that on to my children.

WILL ROGERS,
TWENTIETH-CENTURY AMERICAN RANCHER,
ACTOR, AND HUMORIST

I

WATCHED A SMALL MAN WITH THICK

calluses on both hands work fifteen and sixteen hours a day.

I saw him once literally bleed from the bottoms of his feet, a

man who came here uneducated, alone, unable to speak the

language, who taught me all I needed to know about faith

and hard work by the simple eloquence of his example.

MARIO CUOMO,
U.S. DEMOCRATIC POLITICIAN,
COMMENTING ON HIS FATHER IN HIS 1984 ADDRESS
TO THE DEMOCRATIC NATIONAL CONVENTION

On mornings when my father took me hunting with him

we would get to the woods at about the hour my mother and I had gotten to the Paris hospital in the ambulance with him that morning. But in the woods it would seem like the hour just before Creation. It was as if God said again each day, "Let there be light." Looking just as they must have on the first day, the woods took shape out of the void. The change seemed chemical, like a photographic print in the developer in the dimness of the darkroom, the image appearing out of nothingness, then rapidly becoming distinct, recognizable, familiar. The transformation in my father seemed chemical, too. Perhaps even more in recent years, when illness and disappointment and worry had borne him down, that old boyish wonder of his whenever he went to the woods made a boy of him again. In me he saw the boy he once had been and then for a time he was once again himself. My oneness with him gave me some of his sense of oneness with that world.

WILLIAM HUMPHREY,
TWENTIETH-CENTURY AMERICAN WRITER,
IN *FARTHER OFF FROM HEAVEN*, HIS ACCOUNT OF HIS
FATHER'S DEATH IN PARIS, TEXAS. HE WAS THIRTEEN,
HIS FATHER THIRTY-EIGHT.

I HAVE AN IDEA, NOW, FINALLY,

of what my father was like when I last saw him. Of what he looked like. Of what he sounded like. Even (I count myself lucky for this) a small idea of the kind of man he was. I have a picture anyway of him and me in the last couple of years before he died, a picture in which we are both fairly clear, are clear to each other, seem to touch. But all those years before. There are few pictures, and the ones that still remain seem now so very blurred. I've wondered how clear they were to him.

MICHAEL J. ARLEN,
TWENTIETH-CENTURY AMERICAN WRITER,
ABOUT HIS FATHER MICHAEL ARLEN, NOVELIST AND
FLAMBOYANT PERSONALITY OF THE 1920'S